Bugging In: How to Hunker Down and Survive in an Emergency Situation

by M. Anderson

Disclaimer:

The information contained in this book is for general information purposes only. This book is sold with the understanding the author and/or publisher is not giving medical advice, nor should the information contained in this book replace medical advice, nor is it intended to diagnose or treat any disease, illness or other medical condition.

While we endeavor to keep the information up to date and correct, we make no representations or warranties of any kind, express or implied, about the completeness, accuracy, reliability, suitability or availability with respect to the book or the information, products, services, or related graphics contained book for any purpose. Any reliance you place on such information is therefore strictly at your own risk.

Dedication:

This book is dedicated to my loving wife, who's had to deal with my obsession with backyard chickens, survival skills and homesteading for many long years. I love you sweetie! Thanks for being so understanding.

Contents

What Is Hunkering Down?

Bugging in, also known as hunkering down, is defined as staying in your home and sticking it out during an emergency situation. If you're properly prepped for survival, you'll have everything you need in your home to survive. Unless there's an imminent threat to life or limb, there's no good reason to leave your home to head for a distant location.

Hunkering down should be your first choice when a crisis situation presents itself.

While there has been a lot of literature dedicated to bugging out, which consists of grabbing what you can carry and leaving your home, there surprisingly isn't as much written about bugging in. Maybe it's because the thought of heading for the hills and toughing it out is a sexier concept that sells more books.

The fact of the matter is human beings are creatures of comfort. You'll be far more comfortable remaining in your own home during a crisis situation than you will if you pack up and head into unfamiliar territory. This is especially true if you're heading there with your family. Even if you have a bug out location replete with an underground bunker, your best bet is to stay home whenever possible. That is, unless you're looking for an excuse to test your bunker out. Then, by all means, head there at the first sign of trouble.

What Disasters Should You Prepare For?

The short answer is . . . As many as you can afford to.

The long answer is you need to create a list of all the disasters and emergency situations that could take place in your area and then place them in order from the most likely to occur to the least likely to occur. Once you've created your list, start at the top and prepare for the emergency that's most likely to occur. Once you're done, cross it off the list and prepare for the second most likely disaster. Work your way down the list until you're prepared for as many emergencies as you can afford to prepare for or until you get to the emergencies that are extremely unlikely to take place.

What you're going to find is the first few emergencies are going to be the toughest ones to prepare for because you aren't going to have any of the items you need. After the first couple, you'll already have a lot of the stuff you need in your stockpile and you'll be checking items you already have off of your list instead of buying a bunch of new stuff.

Here's a list of emergencies to get you started:

- Alien invasion.
- Asteroid.
- Biohazardous waste spill.
- Biological agent attack.
- Chemical spill.

- Civil disorder.
- Contamination of the water supply.
- Depression.
- Disease.
- Drought.
- Earthquake.
- Economic collapse.
- EMP.
- Famine.
- Fire.
- Flooding.
- Gas shortage.
- Global cooling.
- Global warming.
- Governmental changes.
- Hailstorms.
- Heat wave.
- Home invasion/robbery.
- Hurricane.
- Nuclear attack.
- Nuclear meltdown.
- Oil shortage.
- Plague.
- Planetary changes.
- Power outage.
- Rioting.
- Sink holes.
- Snowed in.
- Storm.
- Terrorist attack.

- Tornado.
- Tsunami.
- Volcanic eruption.
- War.

That's quite a list, and I'm sure if you think hard enough you can come up with even more stuff to add to it. Sure, a couple of the items on the list are extremely unlikely, but can you definitively state aliens don't exist? You can put that one at the bottom of your list, but you really can't completely rule it out.

Once you've compiled a list, take the list and put it in order from most likely to happen to least likely to happen.

If you live in the SF Bay Area in California, you'd probably list earthquakes as your number one concern. You might list fires as the next item on the list because earthquakes and fires walk hand in hand. If you live in one of the big cities like San Francisco or Los Angeles, civil disorder would probably be high up on your list. On the other side of the coin, a person living in a rural area would probably have civil disorder much lower on their list of concerns.

Your list should be fluid.

In times of economic uncertainty, economic collapse should creep up your list, especially if it looks like your job may be on the line. An announcement of an asteroid headed our way should instantly move asteroid impact to the front of your queue. If you hear a deadly disease is spreading across the nation, guess what your immediate concern should be? You got it, disease.

Prepare for as many disasters as you possibly can, starting with the ones most likely to take place. The more disasters you're able to prepare for, the more likely you are to survive, no matter what happens. If you're prepared for multiple disasters, even if one you didn't prepare for takes place, you're going to be in much better shape than those who didn't prepare for anything.

Personal Disasters: How to Prep for Disasters that Only Hurt You and Your Family

Disaster preparedness is a growing trend. Tens of thousands of preppers join the fold each and every year. I've noticed a disturbing trend amongst these new preppers. They're doing a decent job of preparing for natural and man-made disasters, but are largely failing to prep for personal disasters like unemployment and extended illness.

This failure to prep for personal disaster while preparing for other disasters is a prime example of throwing out the bath water before the bath. You're much more likely to experience a personal disaster than you are a real one. There are tens of millions of people on unemployment and tens of millions more who are unable to work. When was the last time you heard of a natural disaster hitting that many people?

Prepping for personal disaster is similar to prepping for other disasters with one glaring difference. You're going to need money, and a lot of it to survive a personal disaster. While you're largely going to be on your own in an extended emergency situation, you're going to feel like you're on an island being buffeted by high winds in a personal disaster. You're going to be forced to survive with little or no income while banks, creditors and friends and family circle around you with their hands out.

You're still going to need the basics, like food, water and supplies in a personal disaster, but without money, you're soon going to find yourself without power, water, transportation and a place to live. In a real emergency, banks and creditors won't be able to come calling until after the emergency has passed. In a personal emergency, they may call every day. That is, until they come and repossess your belongings, your vehicles and your home.

You're still going to need a stockpile of food, because you may not be able to afford to put food on the table. A 6-month to a year supply of food will serve you well in a personal crisis. Knowing you have food for your family can really ease the burden placed on you when you lose your job or fall ill. It gives you a chance to regroup and rebuild.

In addition to food, you're going to want to build up a 6-month emergency fund that you can use to cover your mortgage and utility bills until you're able to get a job or get on disability. Without this fund, you're going to have a lot more pressure on you. With it, you'll be able to take a bit of time off and won't be forced to take the first job that comes your way.

Prepping for survival means preparing for any disaster life throws your way. Since personal disasters are the most likely disasters to occur, they should be the ones you prep for first.

Bugging Out vs. Bugging In

Should you stay or should you go?

This can be a tough question to answer because disasters rarely follow a set path. There are very few times when you can look at an emergency and definitively state it's best to hunker down or it's time to get out of dodge.

You have to look at the situation at hand and assess it logically, without letting emotion cloud your mind. You may not want to leave your home, but there are times when getting out ahead of the pack is best. There are other times when staying in your home is best.

If you live in a big city in California and hear a radio report that multiple North Korean missiles have been detected over the Pacific, you're probably going to want to bug out. Sure, most of the missiles will probably get knocked down before they reach land, but there's always a chance one will sneak through. Staying in the city places you in danger because you don't know where the missile is aimed. On the other hand, if you live in the sticks, far from any populated area, you're probably better off staying home and waiting to see what happens.

There are a number of natural disasters that take somewhat predictable paths. If you find yourself in the path of a large storm, a forest fire or severe flooding, you're not doing yourself any favors by staying in your home, especially if you have a location you can bug out to where you'll be safe until the worst has passed. All the survival gear in the world won't do you much good if your neighborhood is covered in ten feet of water . . . or lava, for that matter.

Let's look at a situation where the choices aren't as clear. Let's say the country you live in has been hit by a severe drought. You have enough water stockpiled to last 6 months, but know many of your neighbors don't. Lakes, rivers and reservoirs are drying up and it's beginning to look like most of the country is going to end up largely without water, at least until the government is able to formulate a plan. What do you do?

If you live in a remote location, the choice is easy. You stay where you are and live off your water supply until you see what sort of plan the government comes up with. You have time to wait things out a bit to see what happens.

On the other hand, if you live in a big city, you're going to have to make a decision—and fast. This is where things get clear as mud. You could hunker down and stick things out at home. If you go this route, you'd better be prepared to defend yourself from people desperate for water, especially if there are others who know how much water you have stored away. Another option would be to pack up your water and bug out. This is a good option if you have somewhere safe to go and a truck you can use to load your water into, but you're going to have to move quickly. Driving through the city with large amounts of water could be even more dangerous than hunkering down if you wait too long. If you have a remote bug out location with additional water stockpiled, you might end up having to leave the stockpile at home to head to your bug out location.

Bugging out is probably your best choice, but what do you do if you don't have a place in mind to bug out to or a way to pack up your water stockpile if you were to leave?

In this situation, you have to decide whether or not you're safer at home with your water or on the road with little to no water. I'd probably hunker down and try to defend my stockpile. I may even try to work out a deal with an armed neighbor or two where I would offer them water in exchange for help defending the stockpile.

When faced with a tough decision, keep in mind that bugging out doesn't always mean heading off into the wilderness and living off the land. Most of the time you'd be much better off heading to a distant friend or relative's house and crashing out there for a few days. Another option is to rent a motel or hotel room for a while. If you have a big family, things might be a little cramped for a while, but having a roof over your head almost always trumps braving the elements.

If the disaster is local and is confined to a small area, bugging out means leaving the area and removing yourself from the danger presented by the disaster. The only time you need to head into the wilderness is if there's a big enough threat looming that you think things are going to go bad and stay that way for an extended period of time.

War, a deadly disease outbreak, zombie apocalypse, etc. Doomsday scenarios require that you remove yourself from the grid. You'd better be prepared to live off the land. If one of things goes down, you might have to stay bugged out permanently in order to survive.

How Normalcy Bias Can Get You Killed

Don't fall victim to normalcy bias.

People tend to downplay dangerous situations because they don't want to face the truth. They want things to remain normal, so they sit around and pretend things are fine until it's too late. This happens all the time in emergency situations. These are the victims you read about; the people who decided to stay in their homes while everyone around them evacuated.

Normalcy bias is stronger in some people than others.

Most people have a strong will to survive that kicks in and overpowers the normalcy bias when their life is in danger. These people are able to make a logical choice as to when it's time to go. Other people have too strong of a normalcy bias. Lava could be pouring out of the top of a nearby mountain and they'd ignore and carry on as if things were perfectly normal.

There's another name for people with too strong of a normalcy bias. They're called victims. Don't let your bias be the reason you stick around until it's too late.

Questions You Need to Ask Yourself

It's all too easy to panic in an emergency situation. When you panic, you're going to make rash decisions you might end up regretting later. You're going to be in trouble if you let fear guide your decision making process.

It can be tough to think clearly in an emergency situation. For that reason, I've formulated a list of questions you need to ask yourself in order to make a logical decision. Make sure you answer the questions honestly and don't let emotions or normalcy bias cloud your thought process.

Ask yourself the following questions:

- What exactly is the threat and how likely is it to occur?
- If it does take place, what's probably going to happen to my house?
- If I bug in, am I putting my life or the lives of those who stay with me in imminent danger?
- What are the dangers associated with bugging in?
- Am I thinking about staying just because I don't want to leave?
- Am I thinking about staying because I think I can protect my home?
- Is my home more important than my life?
- How long is the crisis likely to last?
- Do I have the supplies I need to survive that long?

- Have I been ordered to evacuate?
- If I am putting my life or the lives of those who stay with me in imminent danger, is bugging out a safer option?
- Where will I bug out to?
- How will I get there?
- Is my bug out location safe?
- If not, is it safer than my current location?
- Do I have the supplies I need at my bug out location?

Use your answers to these questions to guide your decision-making process.

If the threat you're worried about is unlikely to occur, you might want to take a wait and see approach. If there's a fire raging 50 miles to the East and it appears to be headed your way, you should start packing up the stuff you want to take with you and be prepared to leave, but you still have time to wait and see what's going to happen. The fire could be brought under control or it could change directions, at which point you'll be able to stay in the comfort of your own home. If it keeps moving your way and gets within 15 miles of you and appears to be growing, it's time to evacuate. Don't wait until the last minute or you might end up with no way to escape.

If you're looking at an imminent threat that could potentially destroy your house, you're going to be better off bugging out. You don't want to endanger yourself or your party any more than you have to. If the dangers of bugging in exceed those of bugging out, grab your bug out bag and anything else you have time to grab and can fit in your car and leave.

People have strong emotions associated with their homes, especially if they own the house they live in or have lived there a long time. This can lead to foolish decisions like deciding to stick around to try to save the house. While there is the rare person who is able to save their house from disaster, what you don't read about are the victims who ended up dying defending their homes—and their home ended up getting destroyed anyway.

Evacuation orders aren't given lightly.

Deciding to stay when an evacuation has been ordered is rarely a good idea. People who refuse to evacuate are more often than not left behind with no safety net. Once all of the people who want to leave have been evacuated, local police, firemen and medical personnel evacuate as well. You won't be able to call for help if there's an emergency. There won't be anyone to respond until the National Guard is brought in. You could be left for days or even weeks without medical, fire and police services.

If you assess the situation at hand and decide bugging out is the best option, keep in mind there are probably a large number of people just like you who are making the same decision. You need to move quickly and have a contingency plan if you hit the interstate only to find it's backed up for miles in both directions.

The best advice I can give you is to plan ahead. Have a bug in plan in place, along with multiple locations you can bug out to. You'll run out of money long before you cover all of the bases, but the best laid plans attempt to cover as many bases as possible. Taking the time to think things through now while you're level-headed will go a long way towards making sure you don't make a rash decision when the cards are on the table.

Plan Ahead: The 5 Plans You Need to Survive

You're going to need multiple plans in place to ensure you have a good chance of survival. The more planning you do now, the less thinking you'll have to do when a disaster situation presents itself. It's much easier to lay out your plans now when you're mind isn't clouded by stress and fatigue and you're more likely to be thinking clearly.

There are 5 plans you're going to need in order to survive. These 5 plans don't guarantee survival, but they do improve your chances of surviving and being able to rendezvous with your family in the event there's an emergency.

Let's take a closer look at those plans.

Plan #1: The Get Home Plan

Each member of your family is going to need a plan laying out how they're going to get home if they're caught outside the home when disaster strikes. Each person should have a Get Home Bag that will help them make it home in an emergency. Get Home Bags are covered in more detail in the next chapter.

This plan should take into account the places where each person is most likely to be when things go bad. Map out multiple routes you can use to get home and actually travel those routes so you're familiar with them. Let's use your job as an example. If you work 30 miles from your home, there are more than likely going to be a number of roads you can travel to get home. At least once a week, pick a new route and travel that route on your way home from work. It's best to do it on the way home, because you don't know the route and if you get lost, you won't be late for work.

Continue traveling new routes to places you commonly visit until you're so familiar with the routes that you don't need your map anymore. You don't want to be sitting on the side of the road studying a map during a crisis situation. Moving quickly is of utmost importance and you need to be able to change the route you're taking home on the fly.

In addition to mapping out routes you can take while driving, you need to explore the routes you can take on foot. Some emergencies may make driving impossible. There could be cars strewn all over the road or you might want to travel incognito without drawing attention to yourself by driving through the city. A little advance recon may help you identify alternate routes and shortcuts you could take if forced to travel on foot. Try to find routes that will help you stay off the beaten path while avoiding high crime areas whenever possible.

Planning the routes you and your family will travel and ensuring each member of your family has a Get Home Bag are the key tenets of the Get Home Plan.

Plan #2: The ICE Plan

Your ICE plan is your In Case of Emergency plan.

This survival plan covers you and your family members in the event there's an emergency and someone is separated from the group. Each person in the group needs to carry and ICE card with them, either in their wallet or their purse.

Your ICE card should contain the following information:

- Address in town where you can meet if home is destroyed.
- Address out of town where you can meet if town is destroyed.
- Cell, work and home phone numbers of other emergency contacts.
- Cell, work and home phone numbers of parents.
- Emergency medical concerns (allergies, health problems, etc.).
- Home address.
- Police and sheriff contact numbers.

It's also a good idea to set up a social media page like a Facebook group or page where your family can log in and post if they're separated from the group. If phone service is interrupted, the person may be able to locate a computer with an Internet connection. They can log in and post to the page that they're OK, along with their location. Include the URL to this page on your ICE card.

Additionally, each member of the family should wear some form of identification in case they're injured badly and aren't able to identify themselves to first responders. Dog tags work well, as do emergency ID bracelets.

Plan #3: The Bug In Plan

Bugging in requires planning.

You're going to have to look at your home and assess how secure you are in your current location and whether there's anything you could do to ensure you're more secure. You're also going to want to secure as much water and food as you possibly can at the time you bug in and have a plan as to how you're going to dole out your resources.

In a relatively minor emergency like a power outage or a small snowstorm that leaves you snowed in for a couple days, you may opt to take a wait and see approach. If things look like they're going to go back to normal, your plan may be to leave things as-is and not worry about additional security or rationing of resources. There's no good reason to go into panic mode if the situation doesn't call for it.

As an emergency escalates into dangerous territory, you're going to want an action plan.

You may decide to start fortifying your house or you might plan to band up with neighbors who are equally prepared in order to buff up your security. In this stage, you're still taking a wait and see attitude, but you're preparing for the worst. Thing aren't looking good and you could be in it for the long haul.

At some point, things may escalate to the point where they become dangerous. Law and order has gone out the window and you're going to have to protect yourself. It's time to hunker down. You're going to want to plan to hide out and become as invisible as possible while being prepared to defend yourself if necessary.

Your bug-in plan should include how you're going to hand out food and water and how much each member of the household is going to be allotted daily. Setting this up in advance will prevent arguments and bickering when it comes time to dole out supplies.

A well-laid plan gives you a roadmap to follow in an emergency situation. While things might not go exactly to plan, the more things you plan for, the more likely you are to be prepared. Don't just stockpile supplies. Formulate a plan as to how you're going to use those supplies to ensure your survival.

Plan #4: The GOOD Plan

An emergency in which you can't stay in town may present itself. A toxic chemical cloud, a dirty bomb or some other biological threat could make the area you live in uninhabitable. In the event you have to get out of dodge, which is the prepper term for leaving town, you're going to want a plan in place.

Your Get Out of Dodge (GOOD) plan should lay out where you're going to go if you're forced to leave town.

It should include multiple routes you can use, including routes by land, air and sea, if applicable. It should also include planning what you're going to grab on your way out. If you have time, you're going to want to load as much food, water and gear into your car as you can fit. If you don't have time, you're going to have to grab what you can on the way out the door. Identify each route and travel it, so you're familiar with it before you have to use it.

This is especially important when planning routes along trails you're going to travel by foot. Things can change a lot over time and trail that's clearly marked off on an old map may not even exist anymore in real life. You're going to need to know this because it could be the difference between life and death if you set off and can't find your way to your Bug Out Location.

You're going to need Bug Out Bags (BOBs) for each member of your family. These bags should be stored in a hall closet, so they're easy to grab if you have to get out of dodge fast. BOBs allow you to survive in the wilderness on your way to your Bug Out Location in case you have to set off on foot. Without your BOB, you're just lost in the woods. With it, you drastically up your chance of survival.

Your plan should lay out exactly what each member of your family is expected to do in a Bug Out Situation. One person might be tasked with grabbing the firearms and ammo, while another is tasked with rounding up the pets. Practice makes perfect and every second might count, so be sure to run through your bug out drills well in advance.

The Bug Out Living Plan

Once you make it to your Bug Out Location, you're going to need a plan as to how you're going to survive. If things get bad enough that you're heading out to your Bug Out Location, you're probably planning on staying there for an extended period of time. Ideally, you'll have 6 months to a years' worth of food and the ability to create a sustainable food source like an organic garden.

This will take planning in advance.

Since you can't count on having time to grab the food and gear you have stockpiled at home, you're going to need a stockpile of food and gear at your Bug Out Location as well. You'll need the same things there as you needed at home. Ideally, both locations will be stocked with ample supplies to last you over the long haul.

Living off the grid isn't easy, especially for those who are used to having electricity and the instant gratification of buying whatever they want. It can be done, but can be made a lot easier by learning how to live that way well in advance. Plan ahead by spending a week or two at a time at your Bug Out Location a couple times a year in order to learn the ropes. You're much better off learning how to rough it while society is intact. If there's anything you forgot, you'll be able to run out and buy it and add it to your cache. If you wait until you actually have to Bug Out and then realize you forgot something, you're out of luck—or you're going to have to venture into town to find it.

Create a plan and stick as close to it as possible. Planning gives you the best possible chance of surviving an emergency situation. Bugging out is stressful enough as it is. You don't want to further complicate the situation by bugging out without a plan.

The Get Home Bag

Things can go bad fast in an emergency situation. You might find yourself miles from home when disaster strikes. Your number one priority is more than likely going to be getting home to where your stockpile of food and supplies is stored—and to where your family is.

A bad disaster could render roads unable to be driven on. There may be debris scattered everywhere, traffic pileups or jams or even large chunks of concrete and asphalt strewn about blocking your ability to travel by vehicle. If you have to set off on foot, you don't want to do it empty-handed.

You should always have a Get Home Bag in near proximity when you're away from home. A Get Home Bag contains the items you need to help you make it home. You can keep it in the trunk of your car or in a locker at work. I personally prefer to keep my bag in the trunk of my car because I live in earthquake country and worry about an earthquake causing the building I work in to collapse. Stopping to try and grab my Get Home Bag during an earthquake isn't an option and I'd hate to make it out of the building intact only to watch the building collapse with my bag inside.

The first decision you're going to have to make is what type of bag to carry. I've seen everything from backpacks to attaché cases to hefty bags stuffed full of gear. I shook my head in amazement when I saw the last one because the bag was filled to maximum capacity and was ready to burst at the seams. There's no way that bag could have been carried on foot.

A backpack is your best option.

You're going to want to pack light because you may find yourself walking a significant distance, so a regular backpack is probably your best option. Survival stores sell larger backpacks with Urban Camo designs that look cool. You may be tempted to pony up the cash for one of these sweet looking bags. There's just one problem. You're going to want to blend in with your surroundings as much as possible. It's going to be tough to stay off the radar when you have a bag that looks like you're prepared for anything.

A non-descript backpack in a neutral color is your best bet. A normal backpack won't look out of place and will allow you to travel unnoticed. Don't buy one of the cheap bags that are ready to burst at the seams. Spend the extra money and get a bag that's built to last like one of the nicer Jansport bags.

Now that you've picked out a bag, you're going to want some gear for it. Here's the gear you're going to want:

AM/FM radio. Having a radio capable of pulling in news stations will take a lot of guesswork out of getting home.

An empty prescription bottle. There may be roadblocks or groups of military or police officers roving the streets turning people away from your neighborhood. Presenting an empty pill bottle and telling the person in charge you're going to die without your medication may get you a pass into your neighborhood.

Butane torch. You may find yourself in a situation where you need fire. A butane torch will allow you to light that fire even when the wind is blowing.

Cash. Money talks. In an emergency situation, ATMs may be down and credit cards might not work. If you don't have cash, you're going to be out of luck. Keep a couple hundred in small bills in your bag.

Clothes. Keep a change of clothes in your bag that will help you blend into the crowd. Your clothes should be neutral colors. In the winter, you're going to want to carry warm clothes with you. In the summer, you're going to want both cool and warm clothes. You may have to travel at night, so make sure you have clothes appropriate for nighttime travel in your area.

"Dummy" wallet. Keep a fake wallet in your bag with a few bucks and an expired credit card or two. If you're robbed, you can hand over this wallet instead of your real one. Don't keep your real wallet in your bag, because you might get robbed for it at the same time.

First aid kit. Don't overdo it with your first aid kit. Be sure to include bandages, medications you take, aspirin or Tylenol, a tourniquet, surgical scissors, a splint and medical tape.

Gloves. A good pair of gloves will save your hands if you have to do any heavy lifting or work.

Hiking boots. You aren't going to want to walk 20 miles in your dress shoes. Comfortable hiking boots will get you there faster and with less blisters.

Knife. The type of knife you carry is up to you. A survival knife will serve you well, but may be illegal to carry in the area you live. At the very least you're going to want a pocketknife. Get the biggest, sharpest knife you're allowed to legally carry.

Lightweight tarp. You can use a tarp to create a makeshift tent if you need to get out of the elements or bed down.

Map of the city. There's a very good possibility your normal route home will be blocked. Keep a map of the city in your bag and you'll be able to find an alternate route home.

Multitool. This will cover a number of your tool needs, all in one small package. You'll have Phillips and flathead screwdriver attachments, a small saw, a bottle opener, a file and a pair of needle nose pliers, along with any number of other gizmos and doodads. You're going to want a name brand tool like a Leatherman. My wife bought me a multitool from an off-brand and it broke after two days of light use. You're going to need something that's built to last. The cheap stuff doesn't cut it.

Paracord. Carry at least 25 feet of paracord. You never know when you might need to lash something together.

Poncho. This will protect you if it starts to rain.

Pry bar. You never know when you're going to need to pry a door open. A small pry bar will make short work of most doors.

Self-Defense. You're going to want a way to defend yourself. If your state allows it, get a concealed carry permit that will allow you to carry a concealed firearm. A handgun will be ample defense for most situations. If you aren't able to carry a gun, go for one of the less lethal options like pepper spray or a Taser.

Snacks. You're going to want enough snacks to last you at least a couple days. You can include MREs, which are ready to eat meals or you can toss some beef jerky, trail mix and protein bars in your bag.

Solar blanket. You may have to bed down at some point on your way home. A solar blanket reflects your body heat back at you and will keep you warm on a chilly night. It isn't going to keep you from freezing to death in sub-zero temperatures, but it might make you comfortable enough to catch some much needed Z's after a long day of hiking.

Tampons. While the females in your family may need them for obvious reasons, they can be used for a number of purposes. You can use them as makeshift bandages, fire tender, water filters and to stop bloody noses.

Toilet paper. You're going to need a way to wipe your butt, right?

Two LED flashlights. A couple flashlights are better than a single light. LED lights are best because they're bright and the batteries last a long time. You're also going to need a couple extra sets of batteries.

Water. Toss a few large bottles of water in your bag. You should also throw in a LifeStraw, which is a personal water filter that you can use to drink possibly dirty water. It filters at least some of the bad stuff out as you drink. If you run out of clean water, you may have to find other sources of water. The LifeStraw opens up your possibilities to include lakes, ponds, water fountains and any number of other sources of water you wouldn't normally be able to drink from.

Every member of your family who travels away from home should do so with a Get Home Bag in their vehicle.

How Long Should You Be Prepared to Bug In?

That depends. How long do you want to live for if an end-world situation presents itself?

I see survival manuals and government agencies saying you should be prepared to survive on your own for anywhere from a couple days to a couple years. The problem with this line of thinking is it doesn't account for a doomsday event where you're forced to live on your own indefinitely.

Sure, being able to survive for a year is a good goal, but it wouldn't be that much harder to set yourself up to survive indefinitely. If you stockpile enough food and supplies to survive for a year, what are you going to do when your food runs out? You'll be forced to forage, which will put you in danger every time you leave the safety of your home. Each and every time you leave, you'll have to go further and further to get the stuff you need. You'll either have to leave your family at home, which may leave them open to attack, or you'll be forced to take them with you, which leaves your home undefended and ripe for the picking.

While there is definitely a need to stockpile food, I recommend also taking the steps necessary to ensure you have sustainable food sources available if there's an emergency. Start an organic garden and learn how to harvest and collect seeds, keep a chicken coop and learn how to hatch and raise chickens and set up a rabbit hutch and learn how to breed and butcher rabbits. All of these will provide sustainable food sources that you'll be able to turn to when your food stockpile starts to run low.

It's also a good idea to study up on local flora and fauna to see what you'll be able to hunt and gather if need be. If you have squirrels, pigeons or other small game around your home, you can invest in a good pellet gun and learn to shoot it. Sure, you can shoot small game with a rifle or even a handgun, but in an emergency situation ammo can be hard to come by and you won't want to waste it on small game. Save the ammo for defensive purposes and hunting larger game.

At a bare minimum, you're going to want to have enough food and supplies to last 6 months. The more you can stockpile, the better. Be careful not to stockpile so much stuff that you can't rotate your stock and end up having to throw out a bunch of perishable stuff when it goes bad. Ideally, you should rotate your stock periodically and eat or use the older stuff to make room for new supplies.

Don't make the mistake of spending all of your money stocking up in one area while largely ignoring other areas. A supply of food doesn't do you much good if you don't have water to drink and weapons to protect your food supply.

Start off small and stockpile incrementally to ease the damage done to your bank account. Buy an extra can or two of food and an extra bottle of medicine every time you go shopping. Before long, you'll have a huge cache built up without having had to drain your bank account to build it.

Set prepping goals and strive to meet those goals. Start with the goal of being prepared to survive for a week. Next, shoot for two weeks. After that, aim for a month . . . then two month, and so on and so on, until you have a large enough cache to live for a year without outside help.

Don't get so lost looking at the big picture that you don't prep at all.

Some people look at the fact they need a year's worth of supplies and they know they can't afford it, so they don't do anything. Anything extra you can put aside for an emergency is better than nothing at all. Most emergency situations are under control in less than a week. You should at least have enough food and water stockpiled to last that long.

Shelter: Don't Make Any Assumptions

When most people think of hunkering down, they think of doing so in the comfort of their own home. There's only one problem with this line of thinking, and it's a big one. What if your home is no longer standing? Natural disasters can completely devastate a home, rendering it completely unlivable. Tornadoes, earthquakes and fires, just to name a few, can all turn your home into a pile of lumber and sheetrock.

If you're lucky, your home will still be standing. It may have a few holes in it that need to be rebuilt or it may be missing portions of the roof that can be covered by tarps, but at least you'll still have shelter. Your emergency supply should include at least 5 large tarps that can be used to cover damaged areas of your house. Holes in the roof or the siding can be covered with tarps until you're able to rebuild them. This will provide at least some protection from the elements and prevent your house from sustaining further damage during storms.

Be very careful about entering and living in a house that's taken major structural damage. If the walls or support beams are broken or damaged, the house could be on the verge of collapse.

On the other extreme, your house may be completely destroyed. A fire could reduce it (and everything in it) to a pile of ashes. An earthquake could toss it off its foundation and cause it to collapse. A bomb or missile could reduce it to a pile of rubble.

You're going to want a place to stay if your house collapses. If you have a bug out location chosen with a residence stocked with supplies, this would be a good time to head there.

If you don't have a bug out location, you may be better off camping out in your backyard.

You're going to need a tent. If you can afford one, base camp tents like the North Face 2-Meter Dome Tent or the Mountain Hardwear Space Station Tent are a good choice. They're practically indestructible and are built to withstand the elements. The downside is one of these tents will set you back $5K, so they're a pipe dream for most survivalists.

For the rest of us, a normal tent will have to suffice. Make sure you get one large enough to house your whole family. The more space you have, the better. The nice thing about a bug in tent is you don't have to worry about the weight. The furthest you're going to have to carry it is into your backyard. Save the lightweight tent for your bug out bag. You want something heavy-duty that's built to last if you're going to camp in your yard.

Don't store the tent in your house. If your house does collapse, your tent is going to be trapped inside. The tent is intended to be your back-up shelter. Keeping it in your primary shelter defeats the purpose of having a back-up plan.

If you're the least bit handy, you can build a sturdy shed in your backyard to store your tent and back-up supplies. If not, you can buy one. Keep your tent locked away in the shed along with a cache of food and supplies. If your house is destroyed, this may be all you have to survive on, so choose what you put in there accordingly. Those with a large lot should build their shed far enough away from their house that the house can't collapse on it if it's destroyed.

Your shed may be able to serve double duty as shelter if it's big enough. Keep this in mind while building it and include a window or two so you'll have some light if you're forced to use your shed as shelter. Even if your shed is destroyed, it's going to be fairly easy to rebuild as long as you keep the right tools inside.

Survival prepping is all about having as many options as possible. Your house is always going to be your first choice when it comes to shelter, but it isn't guaranteed to be livable after a disaster. Without a backup plan, you could find yourself literally left out in the cold.

Shutting Down the Utilities

Even if your house is still standing, it could be badly damaged. If the damage isn't structural and you aren't being ordered out, you may still be able to hunker down in your home, but you're going to have to be very careful. Everyone in your family should be well-versed on how to shut the utilities to the house off in the event there's an emergency that causes major damage.

The first item on the agenda is finding the shut-off valves in advance and clearly labeling them. When you label them, check them to make sure they're functioning properly and haven't rusted shut or been painted over and are stuck. If they are, you need to contact the utility company ASAP. If you don't know where the shut-off valves and switches are, you can contact them and they're usually more than happy to send someone out to show you.

Once you've identified and labeled the valves, teach every capable member of your family how to operate the shut-off valves. If you aren't home to do it, they're going to need to know how.

Just don't wait until an emergency happens to call. You'll be pretty low on their list of priorities then.

The first valve you're going to want to identify is the natural gas shut-off valve. A gas leak after an emergency can cause fires and if there's enough gas in the air, entire city blocks can be leveled by the resulting explosion. The valve is usually by your gas meter on a pipe coming from the ground. You'll need an adjustable wrench to close it. When the valve is open, the piece you grab with the wrench is in-line with the pipe. To turn it off, turn the valve so it's perpendicular to the pipe.

When you test your valve, don't turn it all the way off. An eighth of an inch should be enough to make sure you're able to turn the valve. Any more than that and all the pilot lights in your house are going to go out and you'll have to call someone out to relight them.

After an emergency, assess the situation and decide whether the gas needs to be turned off. You'll smell gas if it's leaking. If you smell gas, the gas has to be turned off. If there's extensive damage to your house or there's a fire burning in or near your house, you're also going to want to turn off the gas.

Keep a few glow sticks around to use as a light source if you suspect there's a gas leak. They're one of the few light sources that can't touch off a gas fire or explosion if there is a gas leak. Avoid using flashlights and never use a lamp or light that uses combustion to produce light.

If there's a gas leak, turn off the gas and get out of your house until it has time to air out. You don't want to be anywhere near your house if a spark ignites a gas leak and touches off an explosion. Gas explosions are capable of leveling your house and the houses around yours, so make sure you get far enough away from any houses in your neighborhood that you'll be safe.

If you have propane tanks or other fossil fuels that you use, you're going to need to identify the shut-off valves for them as well. The same rules apply, but you need to be extremely cautious because you have a tank of highly flammable material on your property. Whenever possible, stage propane and other fuels as far from the house as possible. You don't want them close enough that a house fire will set off a chain of explosions that does even more damage.

Electrical should be next on the list. If the damage done to your house is so extensive that it's exposed live wires (or you can hear crackling and popping), you're going to need to shut off electrical service to the house.

You need to first find every electrical panel in the house. If there's a handle marked MAIN, that's the one you turn off to cut electricity to the house. Each panel will have to be shut down separately. If there isn't a switch, there could be a fuse labeled main that you have to pull out or a circuit labeled main that you switch off to kill power to the house.

Your best bet is to shut off all of the switches in the panel or pull all the fuses. Shorts have been known to bypass shut off panels. You can never be too safe when it comes to electricity.

Water flooding into your home from broken pipes can quickly make it uninhabitable. If there are broken or leaking pipes, you're going to need to know how to shut the water off.

The main water supply line to your house is usually buried and enters underground into your house from the street. While the area the pipe is buried under isn't marked, there should be a water meter box somewhere along that pipe. In my neighborhood, these boxes are green and are located a foot or two from the sidewalk. These are the boxes that irritate the hell out of your when you're mowing your front lawn.

Inside the box there will be valve that looks like the one you use to shut off your gas. Turn the valve to close it and water to your house is completely shut off.

Water . . . Must Have Water

Hunkering down requires a source of clean water. You can last a week or longer without food, but run out of water and your survival time is reduced to days.

You're going to need water, and a lot of it.

The average person needs at least half a gallon of water a day just to survive. That's almost 2 liters of water per person. When you factor in cooking, hot weather and sanitation, you're going to need closer to 1 gallon of water per person per day. What this means is you're going to need 183 gallons of water per person for a six month supply. A family of five will need more than 915 gallons. When you consider the size of a gallon milk carton, you begin to realize just how much water that is.

It would take a lot of storage space to put away that much water. In addition to storage space, you'd have to buy containers to store it in. You can't use plastic milk cartons because the chemicals from the plastic will start to leach into the water over time, so you'd have to buy containers. At an average cost of $10 each, it would cost $1,830 just for the containers to store that much water—and that doesn't even include the cost of the water.

The good news is you don't have to store that much water. It's a good idea to have at least a month's supply of water stored away, which equates to 31 gallons per person,. Still quite a bit of water, but at least it's a reachable goal for most. Buy a few 55 gallon drums, fill them up and store them in a cool, dark place—preferably somewhere that won't be ruined if one of the containers springs a leak.

Instead of attempting to store thousands of gallons of water, which would take up a ton of space, you have a number of other options that won't take up as much space.

Here are some of your better options:

- **Water filtration systems.** You can purchase water filtration systems that will filter contaminants out of water harvested from potentially unsafe sources. This allows you to collect water from lakes, rivers, streams and many other sources that normally wouldn't be considered safe for consumption. Run the water through the filter and most of the contaminants will be filtered out. There are handheld filters you can buy that work well, but I recommend a larger system capable of filtering more water if it's going to be used while hunkering down.

- **Collect contaminated water and boil or distill it.** Boiling water kills off harmful microorganisms like giardia that can make you sick. Distilling water involves turning it into steam and then condensing the steam back into water and capturing it. This gets rid of harmful microorganisms and impurities in the water. There are home distillation systems available that will allow you to distill water the easy way. Most of them run on electricity, so you're going to need a generator and fuel.

- **Trap rainwater.** There are a number of kits available that will allow you to trap rainwater. If you already have plastic drums full of water, you can hook a kit up to them when they start to run low and trap rainwater in them. Don't forget to treat your rainwater before drinking it.

- **Purification tablets.** These tablets aren't a great option for long-term water purification because they're one-time use tablets and once they're gone, you don't have any way of purifying your water. Keep some in your bug out and get home bags, but there's no good reason to stockpile them in your cache.

- **Bleach.** Liquid household bleach can be used to purify water. You need bleaches that are free of additives like perfumes. The chlorine content should be somewhere in the neighborhood of 5 to 6 percent. You need to add between 10 and 20 drops of bleach per gallon of water you're trying to clean. Add the bleach, let the water sit for a half hour and smell it to make sure it has the slight scent of chlorine. If not add a few more drops and wait another half hour, then check it again.

- **Bath tub storage bags.** These bags are large plastic bladders you place in your tub and fill up with water. The bags will hold between 65 and 100 gallons of water. Buy a couple of bags and keep them in your stockpile. If you hear of an impending emergency, you can fill your bags up for an instant 130 gallons of water. There are also smaller bags available you can use in sinks.

- **Swimming pools.** If you or one of your neighbors has a swimming pool, you may be able to harvest clean water from it. The chlorine in the pool will keep the water inside clean for up to a week, as long as it hasn't been contaminated by flood water or some other contaminant. If an emergency takes place, it may be worth your while harvesting as much water as you can from the pool before it starts to stagnate. When in doubt, always purify your water before drinking it.

The more ways you have to purify water, the better off you'll be. If all else fails, build a fire and boil your water for 10 minutes. That will at least get rid of the bacteria in it. Clean water is a must for survival. It's more important than any other item in your stockpile. Unless you want to die a miserable death, obtaining clean water should be one of your top priorities in the wake of an emergency situation.

It's Getting Cold in Here

Depending on the time of year and the part of the world you're living in, heat may be one of your top priorities. In colder climates, you're going to need a source of heat—and you're going to need it fast.

The human body normally operates at a core temperature of between 98 degrees F and 100 degrees F. Extreme cold causes core temperature to slowly but surely drop. As your core temperature drops below 95 degrees F mild hypothermia sets in. Your body starts shivering and begins to pull blood away from the capillaries of your skin to preserve internal body heat. When the body temperature drops below 90 degrees F, moderate hypothermia sets in. The shivering gets worse, movement becomes difficult and confusion begins to set in. As even more blood is pulled away from the skin, you extremities may start turning blue. At this point, frostbite becomes a real possibility. Once your body temperature drops below 82 degree F, you're in serious trouble. Your respiratory system, heart rate and other bodily functions slow to a snail's pace. Irrational behavior may present itself. People in this stage of hypothermia have been known to hallucinate and take off all of their clothes, which further accelerates the drop in body temperature.

It can take anywhere from a couple hours to a few days for a person to die from hypothermia. Even if you're found before you freeze to death, there's no guarantee you'll survive. The heart is placed under a lot of stress during the rewarming process and can give out. If you do survive, you might lose fingers, toes and even entire limbs to frostbite.

The temperature at which hypothermia sets in depends on a number of factors. An older adult or young child may show signs of hypothermia after spending the night in a room that's 55 degrees F. Skinny and frail people are more susceptible to hypothermia than those with a bit of meat on their bones. Medical conditions like diabetes and drug or alcohol use can also up the risk of hypothermia. So can being wet or out in the wind.

The good news is hypothermia is easy to prevent.
You just have to stay warm.
The bad news is in an emergency situation, this may not be as easy as you might think. When you're hunkered down, there's a good chance you're going to be without electricity. This means your heating system isn't going to work unless you have a back-up power source. Even with a back-up power source, you're eventually going to run out of gas, especially if you're trying to heat your entire home with it.
You can buy heaters that run on kerosene. This fuel source has a long shelf life and can also be used in some lanterns. All you have to do is fill the reservoir and light the heater and you've got a pretty much instant source of heat. Kerosene heaters do produce carbon monoxide in low levels. You need to avoid using them in small spaces where there isn't adequate ventilation. If you are forced to use one in a cramped living space, crack a window to let some fresh air in.
An even better option is to have a wood burning stove or fireplace installed in your home. These will run you upwards of a thousand dollars to have installed, but they

provide a great source of heat when the utilities aren't working. All you need is wood—and that'll be plentiful in a disaster. You can keep a couple cords of wood in your yard as a start. When that runs out, you can scavenge wood from fallen trees, fences and houses that have been destroyed.

The best part is your stove will serve double duty as a place to cook your food. Just make sure you get a stove capable of being used in this capacity. Some don't have this feature.

If you can't afford the cost installing a wood burning fireplace or stove, a barrel stove will provide you with heat for a couple hundred bucks. All you need is a 55-gallon steel drum and a barrel drum stove kit, which will run you around $60 for a good one. Your best bet with a barrel stove is to set it up on a concrete floor because it can get hot and can set a combustible floor on fire. Most people have them in their garage or basement. Make sure you vent your stove to the outside. You don't need to light a big fire for it to provide warmth. A barrel stove can make a room so hot it's tough to stay in it.

When all else fails, grab a few candles and head for a small room like the bathroom. A candle can up the temperature of a small bathroom by 5 to 10 degrees F. This isn't a renewable source of heat, but it may help get you through a cold night.

Speaking of cold nights, you're going to want plenty of blankets, quilts and covers. A few sub-zero sleeping bags can make a huge difference when the temperatures drop. They're designed to keep people in tents warm when the temps drop below zero. They'll do the same thing in your house.

You're also going to want warm clothes. Extra layers equal extra warmth. If the temperature drops too low and you're concerned about the cold, have everyone in the house huddle up together for warmth. Stay out of the wind and stay dry.

Cold nights spent huddled up shivering aren't just miserable—they can be fatal. Make sure you have as many ways to stay warm as you can afford.

Make sure you have a couple battery-powered CO_2 detectors in your stockpile along with batteries to run them. Many of the methods outlined in this section produce CO_2 in conjunction with the heat produced. CO_2 is silent killer and you may not realize it's building up.

Having working CO_2 detectors might just save your life.

How Not to Starve to Death

We, as a nation, have become so reliant on other people providing our food for us that large numbers of people would starve to death if a disaster caused a prolonged interruption to the food supply. Even with food all around, most people don't have the knowledge or wherewithal to hunt and gather their own food.

This wasn't the case not that long ago. In the late 1800's and early 1900's, stores that sold food may have existed, but they were few and far between. Most people weren't reliant on them and had other ways of putting food on the table. Hunting, fishing and farming was the norm back then and were all common methods used to provide sustenance.

Fast forward just over a hundred years and you have a society that's so lazy the vast majority of people don't have the knowledge or desire to raise or grow their own food. And why should we? Everything we could ever want is available at our beck and call. All we have to do is swipe a plastic card through a machine and it's ours for the taking. Our forefathers would be disgusted at what passes for food these days, but we don't care. As long as it's quick and easy, we buy it by the cartload.

Our reliance on the commercial food supply is going to be our greatest downfall if the food supply is ever interrupted. Once store shelves are empty, only a select few are going to have the ability to feed their families. You need to make sure you're one of those few. It isn't hard to raise small animals and grow your own crops of organic food, but it isn't something you want to try for the first time when your life is on the line.

You're going to need a stockpile of food.

Most emergency preparedness agencies recommend at least 3 days of food. This will get you through most emergencies, but what happens when the crisis moves past the 3rd day and your food supply starts to run short? I'll tell you what happens. You're forced to leave the security of your home to forage for food. You won't be the only one doing this, and things can get pretty nasty when people are starving. You're much safer hunkering down and staying out of sight than you are roaming the city looking for scraps the other scavengers may have missed.

If you don't have any food stockpiled at all, 3 days is a good initial goal to shoot for. This much food will get you through most disasters. The key word in that last sentence is *most*. There are a number of disasters where 3 days food will be a drop in the bucket. You'll burn right through that much food in no time at all and end up like the rest of the people who didn't bother prepping.

Once you have a 3 day supply of food, don't stop there. Shoot for a week next. After you hit that goal, move on to a month. Then 3 months, 6 months, 9 months and a year.

The type of food you stockpile is up to you.

You can take the easy (and expensive) way out and buy a stockpile of MREs (Meals Ready to Eat) or freeze dried food. A 3-month supply of MREs will cost you between $1,000 and $2,000. A 6-month supply will cost you between $2,000 and $4,000 and a 1-year supply can run as much as $5,000. Keep in mind these numbers are for food for one person only. If you have a family you're planning on buying food for, you could be looking at $10K or more just for food.

You could also be buying food your family is going to have to choke down. I highly recommend buying small amounts of food at first and taste-testing it before you buy large amounts. I didn't realize how bad some of this stuff actually is until a buddy of mine had to start eating some of his freeze-dried food because it was getting close to the expiration date. It was so bland and nasty that he ended up throwing most of it out. Luckily, I hadn't started building my stockpile yet and was able to learn from his mistake.

If the cost of food has you shaking your head and resigning yourself to starve, there's an easier option. You don't have to buy expensive MRE's or freeze dried foods. These foods are great if you're looking to pack light while backpacking and want to keep the weight of your bag down. They're not so great to eat day-in and day-out for months on end.

To build up a good supply of food without completely breaking the bank, you can buy 3 to 4 extra cans of food every time you go to the store. Depending on what you buy, this will cost you $3 to $5 and will allow you to start slowly but surely building up your food supply. You're going to need a couple thousand calories of nutritious food per person per day. You can get by on less, but your health will begin to suffer. Canned foods will last as long as 5 years in storage before they expire, but you're better off rotating your stock. As you buy new cans, rotate the old cans into your pantry and consume them first.

Dried foods like beans and rice are also good to store. If they're sealed in an airtight container, they have a shelf life of somewhere in the range of 20 years. You can also stock up on ready-made foods like mac and cheese and other boxed foods. Wait until you find a great deal and buy a bunch. 50 boxes of mac and cheese will only cost you $25 bucks if you wait until you find it for $0.50 a box. Taking advantage of great deals is good way to build your stockpile up without spending ridiculous amounts of money.

You can also learn to can and dry your own foods to preserve them. This allows you to take advantage of great deals of produce and meat in order to add to your stockpile. The food you can or dry will last up to a year if stored in a cool, dark place. It's going to take a little extra labor on your part, but is worth it to have your favorite foods available in an emergency.

You're also going to want supplements to ensure you're getting the proper nutrition your body needs. Stockpile a year's supply of multivitamins per person.

Keep your food in a cool, dry place and store it out of the light. Canned foods can be stored on shelves. You're going to want airtight containers for the rest of your food in order to keep insects and rodents away.

Don't forget the manual can opener. You can use the one on your multitool, but it's much easier if you have a regular opener.

Stockpiling food is great.

You should shoot for at least six months of food, preferably a year. In an extended emergency situation this will give you time to get your sustainable food sources established to the point that you're able to live off them.

Speaking of sustainable food sources, you should get started on them now. Plant a small organic garden and learn the ins and outs of growing organic fruits and vegetables. Learning how to save seeds and starting a seed stockpile will allow you to plant a larger garden if the need arises. Seeds collected from hybrid plants won't grow the same variety of plant as the one you collected them from. You need open-pollinated or heirloom seeds to ensure your plants grow true. Otherwise, you never know what you're going to get.

If you have room and it's allowed in the area you live in, keeping chickens and rabbits will provide you with eggs and meat. You're going to need a rooster or two along with your hens in order to get your hens to lay eggs that can be hatched. Otherwise they'll lay eggs that can't be hatched.

Your food stockpile should be big enough to hold you over until you can establish a big enough garden and group of animals to live off of. Starting a garden and raising a small group of animals now will help eliminate at least some of the learning curve associated with living sustainably.

Keep a fishing pole handy, along with a pellet gun or a .22 rifle and plenty of ammo.

You can fish local ponds, lakes and rivers to put dinner on the table and help make your food supply last longer. Small game like squirrels, rabbits and birds can all be hunted with a .22 or a pellet gun. Ammo is cheap for .22 rifles and even cheaper for pellet guns, so make sure you have plenty of it in your stockpile.

You can use your bigger guns for hunting bigger animals like deer and wild boar. Use the pellet gun for the smaller stuff and conserve ammo.

Staying Clean

Water is going to be scarce in an emergency situation, and even if your taps are working, they may not provide clean water. An extended power outage in some areas will equate to dirty water being delivered to people's homes.

Staying clean is of utmost importance if you want to stay healthy. You're going to want to be able to wash up and brush your teeth every day. You'll be more comfortable if you're clean and you'll be less likely to get sick.

Adding unscented baby wipes to your supply cache will give you a means of staying reasonably clean without having to use precious water. You can use a couple wipes a day to wipe yourself down, and you'll be glad you have them if there's an emergency. Buy a couple boxes of wipes and add them to your cache. You'll be glad you did when you're able to stay clean.

Wipe will last a couple years in storage before they dry out. If you add water to dry wipes, they'll be like new again, but that defeats the purpose of having the wipes in the first place. They're relatively cheap and you can get more than 500 wipes for $6 or $7, so be sure to replenish your stock every couple of years.

Don't forget to stockpile other toiletries like toilet paper, toothbrushes and toothpaste. These amenities are things we tend to take for granted because we're used to being able to run to the store whenever we get low.

Deodorant isn't a necessity, but it'll be nice to have, especially if you're forced to huddle together with your family members to stay warm. People can get pretty stinky if they go without bathing for a couple days. Deodorant might make being in the same house as your family tolerable.

Without running water, you aren't going to be able to continue using the toilets in your home. Filling toilets up with excrement and leaving them that way will create unsanitary conditions. You're much better off digging a hole in the backyard and using it.

If you aren't comfortable pooping in a hole in the yard, you can make an emergency toilet out of a garbage can. Use a plastic bag to line the can and do your business in it. Remove the plastic bag from the can and bury it in your yard. If you plan on using this method, you're going to need to stockpile a bunch of plastic garbage bags. You're going to need at least one bag per person per day.

What Do You Mean the Hospital Isn't Open?

Medical attention is something we take for granted. We assume that doctors, nurses and pharmacists are always going to be there when we need them. They will be, but only up to a certain point.

In a bad enough emergency, medical services are going to be limited. Even if the hospital is open for business, you may not want to go there. Bodies could be stacked everywhere, disease could be running rampant and doctors and nurses may be worked to the point of exhaustion. If you show up with something "minor" like a broken arm, you might have to sit for hours or even days before you're treated.

While hospitals may remain open, your family doctor will more than likely be at home attending to his family. So will your pharmacist, which is just as well because pharmacies and drug stores will be ransacked by those looking for prescription medications, both by those with medical conditions and those looking to stock up on drugs they're addicted to.

You're going to need to try to stockpile as much prescription medication as you can. This can be difficult because doctors don't like to prescribe extra medications. There are doctors around who are sympathetic to your needs if you tell them you're stocking up in case of emergency, so it may be worth your while to search around until you find one. You're more likely to get what you want by being honest with your doctor than you are by lying to him or her.

When you build your first aid kit, you're going to need to build it while keeping the fact that you may not have access to medical attention in mind. The thought of performing field surgery on a member of your family may scare you to death, but if it's the only thing that can save your family member's life, you're going to have to do it.

I suggest enrolling in as many first aid and survival classes as you can afford. The more you learn, the better off you'll be. You should also have a field surgery book in your stockpile, along with a couple basic first aid books. The more bases you have covered the better.

Remember, professional medical attention is almost always a better choice. Just because you've read about how to do something or seen it done doesn't make you an expert by any stretch of the imagination. Seek the help of a medical professional whenever possible.

The following list of supplies should give you a good idea of what you need in your kit. You can add to it as you see fit:

- Ace bandages.
- Activated charcoal (for poison control).
- Alcohol.
- Alcohol wipes.
- Allergy medication.
- Aloe Vera.
- Antacid.

- Anti-diarrheal medicine.
- Aspirin.
- Bandages.
- Band-Aids.
- Bandana.
- Bug spray.
- Burn cream.
- Calamine lotion.
- Cold packs.
- Compress dressing.
- Cotton balls.
- CPR mask.
- EpiPen.
- Gauze.
- Gloves.
- Hydrogen peroxide.
- Ipecac.
- Needle and thread.
- Neosporin.
- Pain relievers.
- Petroleum jelly.
- Prescription medications.
- Quick application tourniquet.
- Q-tips.
- Safety pins.
- Saline solution.
- Slings.
- Snake bite kit.
- Space blanket.
- Splints.

- Sunscreen.
- Surgical kit.
- Surgical masks.
- Surgical scissors.
- Tape.
- Thermometer.
- Tweezers.

Some preppers even include advanced (and expensive) medical equipment like dialysis machines and defibrillators. If you're going to include this sort of stuff, make sure you have proper training on how to use it. You can do more harm than good if you use advanced medical equipment improperly.

Again, whenever it's available, you should seek professional medical care.

Bring Out Your Dead

This topic is a tough one to consider because no one wants to think about having to dispose of the dead bodies, especially those of friends, family members and neighbors. The reality is, in a bad enough emergency, there could be bodies piled up everywhere.

So what do you do when calls to funeral home or county medical examiner go unanswered?

The answer depends on how you feel about disposing of the bodies. If the dead person is someone you know and want to give a proper burial, you can bury them in the ground. This method is clean and allows you to somewhat quickly get rid of a body or two, but digging a deep enough hole to bury people in can be backbreaking labor.

We've all heard the term "6 feet under" when it comes to burials. This term dates back to the days of the plague when bodies were required to be buried that deep to prevent transmission of disease. You can breathe easy. You don't have to bury bodies that deep to prevent transmission of disease. 2 to 3 feet is usually more than enough.

The body doesn't have to be placed in a coffin. In fact, burying a coffin is going to be even more work because you're going to have to dig a hole big enough to fit the coffin into. You can simple roll the body into the hole and cover it with dirt. If you can't bring yourself to do that, wrap the body in cloth before burial. It isn't going to matter in the long run.

While burial is a good option for a limited number of bodies, it isn't always possible, especially if you have multiple bodies on your hands. One thing's for certain; you can't leave the bodies lying around to rot. They'll stink the place up and become unsanitary. You can use the following methods to dispose of bodies:

- **Cremation.** Burning bodies can make them sanitary. While you probably aren't going to have use of a funeral home's cremation oven, you can accomplish the same thing by stacking logs on top of and around the body and lighting them on fire. It's going to take some time to get the fire hot enough to reduce a body to ashes, but it can be done.
- **Burial at sea.** If you have a large body of water like an ocean or big river, you can bury the body at "sea." Be aware that smaller bodies of water can be contaminated if you use this method. Don't dump bodies in your drinking water source. You can also take the body out into the middle of a large lake, weight it down and sink it.
- **Dissolve it.** Caustic chemicals can be used to dissolve the body.
- **Remove it.** When all else fails, remove the body from the area and dump it somewhere you aren't going to return to. This may be your only viable option if you have large numbers of dead you have to get rid of.

I want to make something very clear here. The methods of body disposal outlined in this book are more than likely illegal in your jurisdiction. They should only be used in a survival situation where rule of law has been suspended.

Security: How to Stay Safe When You Can't Call the Cops

The sad but true reality is violent crime, and crime in general for that matter, increases when there's a large disaster. If first responders are still around, they're often overwhelmed and have to pick and choose the calls they respond to. You may not get an answer if you're forced to call 911, and if you do, there's no guarantee they'll be able to send someone out.

Criminals know this and seek to take advantage of the situation.

Opportunists will riot and rob houses they believe to be empty or that they think contain valuable items. In a prolonged crisis, you don't just have to worry about the criminals; you also have to worry about the desperate masses who didn't prepare. Fear is a powerful motivator and people who wouldn't normally be a threat may do things you wouldn't expect.

You're going to be diligent about ensuring your home is as safe and secure as possible. You can attack this from three fronts:

- **Lock down the neighborhood so it's difficult for outsiders to get into.**
- **Make your home as hard to get into as possible.**
- **Arm yourself with weapons you can use for self-defense purposes.**

The first security items is going to require like-minded neighbors who are as prepared as you are for an emergency situation. If your neighbors aren't prepared or aren't willing to help, you might have to skip to step 2. If your neighbors are willing to help, the best thing you can do to secure your house is to secure your neighborhood from outsiders coming in. Setting up roadblocks to keep traffic out and watch guards to turn would-be looters around before they can get in can keep all the homes in the neighborhood safer than each family being only responsible for their own safety.

Obviously, this is going to take a lot of coordination and even more cooperation to implement correctly. For those situations that aren't bad enough to require roadblocks and guards, you can set up a neighborhood watch program where each neighbor commits to looking out not only for themselves, but for those around them as well.

The second step requires upgrading your home so it's as hard to get in as possible. You want to ensure all of your outside doors are solid metal doors capable of being bolted shut. As an additional layer of security, you can mount door bars on the outside doors. You can make things even harder by planting thorned bushes in front of each of the windows and letting them grow wild.

While you may not want to live in a house that has bars across the windows and solid barred screens covering all of the doors, would-be robbers are going to take one look at a barred-up house and move on to the house down the street that's easier to get into. Even if they attempt to get in, you'll have plenty of time to fight them off.

A big guard dog or two will deter all but the most determined of thieves from entering your yard—and you'll hear the racket if they do enter. I have two dogs. One I plan on keeping outside and one on the inside. Criminals are going to have to get past both of my dogs first—at which time they'll have to deal with me.

Here are more tips for staying safe:

- **Install solar-powered flood lights around your house**. The more the better. When a criminal approaches your house at night, the lights will come on. If they stick around, you'll be able to see where they are and what they're up to long before they see you.

- **Let the world know how secure your house is.** Put cameras up at all four corners of your house. Even if they're fake, criminals won't know this. You should also put up a sign from a burglar alarm company and a "Beware of Dog" sign.

- **Don't leave unless you absolutely have to.** An emergency is no time to let your kids run around and play in the front yard. If you have a secure back yard, let them out there for a while each day. You're much better off—and less exposed— if you stay in your house.

- **Trust no one.** Even people you know can turn on you in an instant if you turn them away when they request help. Never open your doors to anyone you don't know, and be extremely cautious opening them for people you do know.

An open door bypasses a lot of the security you have in place.

You're going to need guns.

The bad guys will have them, and the only thing that fights off a bad guy with a gun is a good guy with a gun. In a lawless society, those with the guns are going to rule the world.

For home defense purposes, I recommend at least owning a pistol and a shotgun. You should have guns for every able-bodied member of your household. The more controlled fire you can put on a criminal or group of criminals, the more likely they are to give up. Having multiple people walking around armed can be a great deterrent. Criminals want easy targets and aren't going to want to get into a firefight.

The pistol can be used for mid-range combat and the shotgun can be used if things get up close and personal. The pistol can be whatever caliber you're comfortable with. The higher-powered handgun rounds are capable of shooting through walls, so exercise caution if you don't know where the other members of your party are.

A scoped rifle will serve you well if you get into a firefight where there are people shooting at you from a distance. Dial in your scope ahead of time and practice hitting targets at different distances.

There's one more weapon I recommend adding to your arsenal. In skilled hands, it can be every bit as deadly as a firearm. That's a bow and arrow. A good bow is easyto shoot, it's almost completely silent and you can reuse the ammo time and time again. Keep extra bowstrings on hand

and buy as many arrows as you can afford to stockpile. A bow and arrow can be used to take down enemy combatants, small game and even larger game like deer and elk—and you can do so without announcing to the world that you're around. When silence is golden, a bow and arrow is worth its weight in gold.

Train with your weapons as much as possible. Don't just train standing still and aiming at a target. Anyone can hit a target shooting like that. Being able to shoot while moving will give you the upper hand in a fire fight. Practice shooting while on the run and learn how to shoot while hiding behind cover. A moving target is much harder to hit than a stationary one. If you can learn to shoot while moving, you'll be much efficient and less likely to take damage during combat.

The world's a dangerous enough place when there is law and order. Remove fear of prosecution and it becomes even more dangerous. If there's no fear of prosecution, the only thing stopping a criminal from robbing you blind is fear of bodily harm. That's a powerful deterrent right there, so make use of it.

How Alcohol and Tobacco Could Save Your Life

In a bad enough emergency, paper currency could be rendered useless. Precious metals like gold, platinum and silver might be of value, but they might not. You're going to want to stockpile some items that are going to be as good as gold in a prolonged emergency.

Vice items might be your best bet.

Cigarettes, chewing tobacco, alcohol, etc. all might be worth their weight in gold if supplies run low. People are going to want these items. Some people are going to have intense cravings for them. Liquor stores and smoke shops are going to be pillaged and picked dry within weeks of an emergency. When supplies run out there, people are going to have to start looking elsewhere for the items they want.

Having a good stock of those items puts you in a position of power, but only if you have the ability to protect yourself if someone attempts to forcibly take those items from you. As long as you're able to protect your cache, you can leverage it to get anything you want. If you start to run out of something crucial to your survival, you can use vice items to barter with people who have the supplies you need.

In a world where money is of no value, the currency is going to be items people either need or want. Vice items are going to be high on both the need and want list once people run low. Stock up on cheap alcohol and tobacco today and you might find yourself in a position of power in a crisis.

If you can't bring yourself to stockpile vice items that take advantage of people's bad habits, you can stockpile chewing gum and candy. They'll both be in high demand as well.

Why a Generator Might Not Be a Great Idea

At some point in your prepping, you're probably going to look at your stockpile and think about adding a generator and enough fuel to run it for an extended period of time. While a generator is a great tool to have, it isn't going to be the lifesaver some people think it is. In fact, it could put your life in danger.

A generator is great for short-term emergencies.

You can use it to provide lights, power to cook with and even power to keep your fridge cold so your food doesn't spoil. It can also be powered up to allow you to run power tools you can use to rebuild your shelter if it's been damaged. It will serve you well for the first few days of an emergency and is a worthwhile investment solely for this reason.

As more time passes, your generator could end up being more trouble than it's worth.

For one, you're going to need gas for it. A lot of gas. A generator uses between 8 to 20 gallons of gas a day depending on the size of the generator. In two weeks you could use as much as 280 gallons of gas if you run your generator 24 hours a day. You can only stockpile so much gas. A couple weeks supply of gas is probably the most you're going to want to keep around for your generator—and that's pushing it. When the gas runs out, you either have to find more gas or turn the generator off.

As days turn into weeks, the people who didn't prep (and the people who did, but only prepped for a couple days) are going to start getting desperate. They may group up and start roving around in packs looking for supplies. These desperate people may be willing to resort to violence to get the supplies they need.

Nothing screams "I prepared for this emergency and you didn't" louder than the hum of a running generator reverberating through your neighborhood. In a time when you want to stay under the radar, you're going to be calling people in like moths to a flame. They'll either come begging for help or looking to take what you have. Either way, you're going to end up attracting unwanted attention.

In an extended emergency, you're going to have to learn to live without electricity sooner or later anyway. It might as well be sooner rather than later. Keep a generator on hand for those times when you absolutely have to have power, but avoid running it constantly.

You don't want the whole neighborhood to know how prepared you are.

There's a Better Way to Make Sure You Still Have Power

You can have power without announcing to your neighbors that you're living the high life while they're withering away. The way to do this is through judicious use of solar power. While an extensive set of solar panels on your roof or in your yard is going to be a dead giveaway, there are smaller portable options you can use to power lights, power tools and other electronics.

For less than $1,000 you can get a portable solar generator system that's the size of a suitcase. You can set it out in the sun during the day and use it as a power source at night. These systems are capable of storing 150+ watt hours of power, which can run LED lights for days on end on a single charge and other electronics and tools that draw a heavier load for a few hours at a time. You can use it to power portable fans, heaters and even your iPad or phone.

Smaller solar kits are available that can be used to charge electronics. These kits can charge a cell phone battery in a matter of hours. Some of them can run small tools and devices for short periods of time.

If you have a couple thousand dollars burning a hole in your pocket, you can buy a portable system that consists of a few movable panels and a charging pack. These kits charge in 4 to 6 hours and can provide enough power to run appliances for hours on end. The batteries last anywhere from 5 to 10 years and can be charged thousands of times. Additional panels can usually be added to speed up charging times.

The nice thing about these portable units is you can set them up and take them down to your heart's desire.

It's Too Dark in Here

Light can be both a very good and very bad thing.

You're going to want at least some light at night. Stumbling around in the dark isn't fun and it can be dangerous if you trip and fall over something and get hurt. If you have a wood burning fireplace, the ambient light provided by the fire may be enough to light the room up just enough so it isn't too dark.

If you still have running water and your bathroom is in working order, you're going to need a source of light in there. An LED lamp or lantern that runs on batteries can give you enough light to see when you go to the bathroom. Make sure you stock up on batteries, so you'll have enough to last you through the emergency.

Those who don't have a wood-burning fireplace are going to need a few LED lanterns. That way, you can keep one in the room where everyone is sleeping and the other one can be used to go to the bathroom and for perimeter checks.

Keep multiple sources of light around the house in case of emergency. I have flashlights in every room in the house. That way, if I'm in a room and the lights go out, all I have to do is go to the drawer or cabinet where I keep the flashlight instead of having to stumble through the house trying to remember where I left the flashlight last time I used it.

Light is good for helping you find your way around at night. It's bad because it can help other people find you at night.

If you're trying to stay out of sight, you're going to have to do one of two things when it gets dark—institute a strict lights out policy once the sun goes down or seal your house up tight so there are no leaks. This means boarding the windows up tight and covering all holes to ensure no light leaks out that can be seen from outside the house.

Avoid staying in a room that's lit up with bright light. If something happens and you have to go out into the dark, you aren't going to be able to see for a few moments. In a combat situation, this could be the difference between light and death. You want the room you're in to have a bit of ambient light so you can see, but not be so lit up you won't be able to see anything if you have to cut the lights out.

Sealing Yourself In: Protecting Yourself from Chemicals and Radiation

Be it from a dirty bomb, a nuclear power plant accident or a bioterrorist attack, there may come a time when you need to seal your home and shelter-in-place. When the order comes, you're going to need to get your house sealed up, and it's going to need to be done quickly.

Depending on the agent released and how much of it was dispersed, staying in your home may largely shield you from exposure. You're going to need to stay inside for as long as it takes for the agent or radiation to disperse (or decay, as is the case with radiation). This could be a matter of days, weeks or even months. The longer you're prepared to seal yourself in, the better off you'll be.

Ideally, you'll have a centrally located room in your house that doesn't have very many windows. If you have a room that's free of windows, like an underground basement, that's probably your best bet. Some people have underground bunkers built in their backyards or at their Bug Out Location into which they can scamper when there's an emergency. Other people bury shipping container to which they hook up a ventilation system. These are good places to shelter-in-place because they're hidden away and are largely sealed off to the outside. Make sure your ventilation system is designed to keep fall-out from getting in and install a HEPA filter capable of filtering out biological agents.

If you're outside when the attack takes place, cover your face with a shirt or something else made of fabric. This will filter out at least some of the particulate contamination.

When you get to your shelter, take off your clothes and leave them outside. You don't want to bring anything into your shelter. If it's too cold to remove all of your clothes outside, take off at least the top layer of clothing. As much as 85 to 90 percent of the contamination is going to be stuck to your clothes. You should also leave your shoes outside. Take a shower as soon as you get inside to wash away as much of the contamination as possible.

Be sure to turn off all air systems that bring air in from the outside.

Close all windows, vents, etc. Head to the room you plan on staying in and seal up the room. Place heavy plastic sheeting over any vents, windows, ducts and doors and duct tape them in place. You can't leave the room sealed like this for long periods of time, but a few hours should be fine. If you leave the room sealed up airtight for too long, you can suffocate. Only leave it sealed until the worst has passed.

Tune in to the radio to find out what's going on and how bad things are to get an idea of how long you're going to have to shelter-in-place. A laptop with an Internet connection can also be used to glean useful information. You're probably going to see conflicting reports. Take everything you read and see with a grain of salt and don't evacuate until you feel it's safe to do so.

To further up your chances of survival, you can purchase NBC (Nuclear, Biological, Chemical) or Hazmat suits that you can put on to protect your body from particulate exposure. These suits can keep particles out to 0.1 micron in size.

Hazmat and NBC suits aren't going to do you much good without a gas mask with the proper filters. Make sure your filter is rated for Nuclear, Biological and Chemical attacks or you might find you aren't safe even while wearing the mask. In a heavily contaminated area, your filters are going to last less than an hour. You're either going to have to have extra filters on hand, so you can change them when breathing through them feels labored because they're clogged with particulate, or you're going to have to get out of dodge before the filters you have on hand fail.

Filters typically have a shelf life of 3 to 5 years. After that, they start to degrade and lose effectiveness. Replace your filters regularly. Your life might depend on it!

Back to the Stone Age

I'm of the opinion you should prepare for the worst. That way, if something less than the worst takes place, you'll be more than ready for it.

Short of an end-world scenario where everyone but a select few is destroyed in a heartbeat, one of the toughest disasters to recover from would be a nuclear bomb being detonated in the atmosphere. The Electro Magnetic Pulse (EMP) created by such a detonation could render electronic devices across a wide area completely useless. There's speculation that high-powered EMP weapons are under development that could render the electronics of an entire country useless.

Think about the impact an EMP that big could have.

Communication, food, water, banking, travel, finance, entertainment, information systems, defense shields, weapons systems and computer systems all would be rendered completely useless by such a weapon. It would take years to rebuild and would render the entire country incapable of communicating and properly defending itself. It's estimated that hundreds of millions of people could die from such an attack. A large percentage of these deaths would be because people are unprepared and would starve to death before the infrastructure could be rebuilt.

A lot of the prepping you do for disaster will prepare you for an EMP attack. The food, water and non-electronic supplies you have will all still be good after such an attack. All of your electronics, communications devices and such will be rendered inoperable by a strong enough attack. Many vehicles will be crippled. Keep this in mind when creating your stockpile and go heavy on the hand tools and non-electronic items. Keep hard copies of important books, papers and documentation on hand. If you're storing everything on your iPad, laptop or PC, it could all become inaccessible if an EMP hits.

If you have electronic items you want to protect, a Faraday cage can be built to protect them. A small Faraday cage can be built for less than $20.

There are tutorials online that show you how to build one from a metal garbage can, aluminum foil and a cardboard box. You won't be able to fit anything big into it, but you can store a few handheld radios, so you'll still be able to communicate after an attack.

Don't forget to store the batteries you need to operate your electronics in the cage as well. There hasn't been enough testing on EMP pulses to definitively state batteries won't be damaged if they aren't protected. Better safe than sorry.

How likely is an EMP attack?

Probably not likely, but a possibility. And it's one that could render a lot of your prepping obsolete in one fell swoop while sending entire countries hundreds of years back in time.

Prepare for the worst and hope for the best. The more you're prepped for, the better off you'll be.

Communication: What to Do When the Phones Won't Work

We've become so reliant on our cell phones we tend to forget there are other forms of communication that can be used in an emergency. Survival communication consists of having two types of communication: One-way communication and two-way communication.

One-way communication is a means through which you can gain information on what's going on in the outside world. You can't use it to contact people if you need help, but you can use it to see whether it's safe to return to society.

A television with an antenna is one form of communication. Even if cable or satellite TV isn't working, there may be television stations broadcasting over the air that you can pull in with an antenna. Of course, you have to be close enough to civilization in order for you antenna to draw in a signal. You also have to have ample power to run your television.

A better choice may be an AM/FM radio. You can get a battery-operated radio that runs on a couple AA batteries. These tend to be small radios and would be a good choice for a Bug Out Bag. You can also add a bigger radio with a larger antenna that's capable of pulling a signal in from a much greater distance to your cache. I'd also recommend a hand crank radio that can be powered up by turning a crank on the side of the radio.

Scanners can be used to monitor emergency response team and police communications. There are handheld and desktop versions available and you can even download apps on your smartphone that allow you to monitor communications. Scanners can also be used to pull in AM and FM radio channels.

Two-way communication means being able to get in touch with others and staying in touch with members of your party when they're out and about.

Cell phones are the number one form of two-way communication in the world today. An emergency could knock out cell towers and satellites or systems could be overloaded with people trying to communicate. If you've ever tried to call someone during an emergency and instead received a message stating the call couldn't be connected as dialed, you know how frustrating it can be. You can count your cell phone as a communication device in an emergency, but you shouldn't count on it being your only form of communication. Phone service is notoriously unreliable during crisis situations.

Add other forms of two-way communication to your stockpile and you'll be able to communicate with the outside world no matter what.

Walkie talkies will allow you to communicate with members of your party from a distance. Family Radio Service (FRS) radios are good up to a distance of a couple miles and have a limited number of privacy channels available. General Mobile Radio System radios are more powerful and have more privacy channels available, but require a license to operate. The license costs less than $100 and is good for 5 years. GMRS radios can communicate at distances of up to 25 miles for some of the better radios.

Citizen Band (CB) and HAM radios are another option for communication that will allow you to legally communicate with others and to coordinate emergency services. Check your local laws and regulations to see if licenses are required to operate on the radio frequencies you plan on use. A radio with the ability to scan channels is capable of searching for transmissions across multiple frequencies. This can be invaluable if you're searching for other survivors. Make sure you learn in the ins and outs of operating your radio well in advance and keep a list of channels you might be able to use during an emergency taped to your radio. This might be your only form of communication with the outside world in an emergency.

HAM radios are a good choice for communication over long distances. A good HAM radio can be invaluable at a bug out location because it might be the only communication tool capable of communication from your location.

Communication is going to be an important part of survival after an emergency. The more methods of communication you have available, the better off you'll be.

Appendix #1: Supply List

Here's a list of the supplies you're going to want to start stockpiling. If you haven't started prepping and don't have any of the supplies stockpiled already, you're going to feel overwhelmed at first. Don't worry. We all went through this when we first started.

Start slow and pick up an item here and there as you can afford it. Before long, you'll start building up a respectable stockpile. One thing's for sure. Having at least some supplies is better than having no supplies. Don't get caught empty-handed.

Tools/Gear:

- 55-gallon drums and rainwater traps.
- Apple cider vinegar.
- Baby powder.
- Baby supplies (if you have a baby).
- Baking soda.
- Bandanas.
- Batteries.
- Binoculars.
- Bird seed.
- Bleach.
- Board games.
- Bolts.
- Books.
- Brillo pads.
- Buckets.
- Bullet-proof vests.

o Butane lighters and fuel.
o Buttons.
o Camp stove.
o Can opener.
o Candles.
o Carabiners.
o Chain.
o Citronella candles.
o CO_2 detectors.
o Cold weather gear.
o Compass.
o Condoms (can be used to store water and, well, you know).
o Dental floss.
o Deodorant.
o Detergent.
o Dutch oven.
o Extra cell phone, charged batteries and solar charger.
o Extra glasses and contacts.
o Fertilizer.
o Fire extinguishers.
o Fire steel.
o First aid kit.
o Fishing line, hooks, bobbers, lures and pole.
o Flashlights and spare bulbs.
o Garbage bags.
o Garden tools.
o Gasoline.
o Generator.
o Glow sticks.

- o Hand pump.
- o Hand tools.
- o Hatchet.
- o Heavy plastic sheeting.
- o ICE cards.
- o Ice chests.
- o Inflatable mattresses.
- o Kerosene heaters.
- o Knife sharpener.
- o Lanterns, mantels and fuel.
- o Laptop with satellite card.
- o Lime.
- o Locks (various sizes).
- o Lumber and plywood.
- o Magnifying glass.
- o Maps (both road and topographic).
- o Matches.
- o Mosquito netting.
- o Motor oil.
- o Mouse traps.
- o Multitool.
- o Nails.
- o Night vision binoculars.
- o Oil lamps, wicks and oil.
- o Paper towels.
- o Paracord.
- o Paraffin wax.
- o Pens and paper.
- o Personal documents.
- o Pet food.
- o Pet supplies.

- o Plastic bags.
- o Playing cards.
- o Pocketknife.
- o Radios (two-way and AM/FM).
- o Rain gear.
- o Razors.
- o Safety glasses.
- o Saw and saw blades.
- o Screws.
- o Seeds.
- o Sewing kit.
- o Shampoo.
- o Shoe laces.
- o Sleeping bags.
- o Slingshot.
- o Solar lights.
- o Solar power generators.
- o Space blankets.
- o Spare keys to house and vehicles.
- o Spark plugs.
- o Spray paint.
- o Super glue.
- o Survival knife and sheath.
- o Tarps.
- o Tents.
- o Tobacco.
- o Toilet paper.
- o Toolbox full of common tools (wrenches, sockets, screwdrivers, Allan wrenches, etc.).
- o Toothbrushes and toothpaste.
- o Towels.

- o Tub bags for water storage.
- o Twine.
- o Vitamins.
- o Water filtration system.
- o WD-40.
- o Wheelbarrow.
- o Wipes.
- o Wire.
- o Wood-burning stove.

Defense/Hunting:

- o Blow gun and darts.
- o Bore snake.
- o Bow and arrow (or crossbow and bolts).
- o Cleaning kits.
- o Extra magazines.
- o Handgun, holster and ammo.
- o Hunting rifle (or AR-15) and ammo.
- o Lube.
- o Pellet gun and pellets.
- o Repair parts.
- o Shotgun and ammo.

Get Home Bag:

- o AM/FM radio.
- o An empty prescription bottle.
- o Backpack.
- o Beanie.
- o Butane torch.

- o Cash.
- o Clothes.
- o Cold weather clothes.
- o Duct tape.
- o "Dummy" wallet.
- o First aid kit.
- o Gloves.
- o Hiking boots.
- o Knife.
- o Lightweight tarp.
- o Map of the city.
- o Multitool.
- o Paracord.
- o Poncho.
- o Pry bar.
- o Self-Defense.
- o Snacks.
- o Solar blanket.
- o Tampons.
- o Toilet paper.
- o Two LED flashlights.
- o Water.
- o 25 water purification tablets.

First Aid:

- o Ace bandages.
- o Activated charcoal (for poison control).
- o Alcohol.
- o Alcohol wipes.
- o Allergy medication.

- o Aloe Vera.
- o Antacid.
- o Anti-diarrheal medicine.
- o Aspirin.
- o Bandages.
- o Band-Aids.
- o Bandana.
- o Birth control.
- o Bug spray.
- o Burn cream.
- o Calamine lotion.
- o Cold packs.
- o Compress dressing.
- o Cotton balls.
- o CPR mask.
- o Emergency dental repair kit.
- o EpiPen.
- o Eyedrops.
- o Gauze.
- o Gloves.
- o Hydrogen peroxide.
- o Iodine.
- o Ipecac.
- o Needle and thread.
- o Neosporin.
- o Pain relievers.
- o Petroleum jelly.
- o Prescription medications.
- o Quick application tourniquet.
- o Q-tips.
- o Safety pins.

- o Saline solution.
- o Slings.
- o Snake bite kit.
- o Space blanket.
- o Splints.
- o Sunscreen.
- o Surgical kit.
- o Surgical masks.
- o Surgical scissors.
- o Tape.
- o Thermometer.
- o Tweezers.

Vehicles:

- o 4 X 4 truck.
- o ATV.
- o Boat.
- o Dirt bike.
- o Motorcycle.
- o Small, non-descript car.
- o Small plane.
- o Snowmobile.

Appendix #2: Survival Skills You're Going to Need

All that gear isn't going to get you anywhere if you don't know how to use it. You're going to want training in the following areas in order to up your chances of survival:

- Animal husbandry.
- Archery.
- Combat skills.
- CPR.
- Firearm handling.
- Fire starting.
- First aid.
- Fishing.
- Home repair.
- Hunting.
- Knot-tying.
- Local flora and fauna.
- Organic gardening.
- Stress management.
- Urban survival.
- Weapons training.
- Welding.
- Wilderness survival.

Appendix #3: Step-by-Step Guide to Getting Prepped

You asked for it and you got it—a step-by-step guide to getting ready for disaster. Following these steps may not prepare you for anything, but they'll get you ready for most disasters. You don't need to follow these steps in order. In fact, you can do a lot of them at the same time to speed things up. What's important is that you get started today and continue prepping into the future.

If you already have some of the gear or skills listed, you can check it off the list and move on to the next step.

Here's the list of stuff you need to get done:

- o Create Bug In plan.
- o Create an evacuation plan for your home that identifies all exits. If you have a two-story home, make sure you have escape ladders at the ready. Practice evacuating from various rooms of the house until it's second nature.
- o Identify utility shut-off valves, label them and train everyone in the family on how to use them.
- o Designate a space in your house for storage. Make sure the floor is properly supported to handle the extra weight.
- o Create a household budget. Identify areas where you're spending unnecessary money. Tighten things up and use the extra money to start prepping.

- o Start reading books and websites on prepping.
- o Create Get Home Plan that identifies multiple routes home for each member of the family.
- o Put together Get Home Bags for the entire family.
- o Create ICE cards for the family and formulate your ICE plan.
- o Build up a 3-day supply of water.
- o Build up a 3-day supply of food.
- o Build up a 3-day supply of your other supplies.
- o Acquire at least one weapon you can use to defend your cache.
- o Take firearms training course. If you already know how to safely use and handle your firearm, take an advanced course.
- o Gather first aid supplies.
- o Take basic first aid and CPR courses.
- o Start taking survival skills courses as you have time.
- o Get in shape, so you can walk home in an emergency.
- o Take a hiking trip and camp out for a couple days.
- o Start an organic garden and learn how to save seeds.
- o Start a chicken coop and learn how to hatch and raise chickens.
- o Start a rabbit hutch and learn how to raise rabbits.
- o Build up a 7-day supply of water.
- o Build up a 7-day supply of food.

- Build up a 7-day supply of your other supplies.
- Put a plan in place to start rotating your stock of perishable supplies.
- Practice sheltering-in-place and sealing off a room.
- Get with your neighbors and see if they're willing to create a neighborhood watch/lockdown program.
- Install floodlights around your house.
- Learn how to start fires using the various methods of fire-starting, including friction fires.
- Create a Bug Out Bag you can use to evacuate.
- Formulate your GOOD (Get Out of Dodge Plan).
- Identify a Bug Out Location and start stocking it with supplies.
- Identify routes you can use to get to your Bug Out location both by vehicle and on foot. Travel those routes.
- Formulate your Bug Out Living Plan.
- Build up a 1-month supply of food, water and supplies at your home and Bug Out location.
- Acquire communications gear and learn how to use it.
- Purchase generator.
- Acquire a bow and begin stockpiling inexpensive arrows. Learn how to use the bow to hunt and for defensive purposes.
- Acquire additional weapons to protect your cache and for hunting purposes and start stockpiling ammo.
- Learn how to fish and hunt locally.

- o Install wood stove or barrel stove and learn how to use it.
- o Acquire your Concealed Carry Permit, if your state allows it.
- o Test your Bug Out Location by bugging out for 1 week. Adjust your plan and supplies accordingly.
- o Build up a 3-month supply of food, water and supplies at your home and Bug Out location.
- o Purchase water filtration devices.
- o Purchase solar backup power.
- o Build up a 6-month supply of food, water and supplies at your home and Bug Out location.
- o Begin purchasing Bug Out vehicles.
- o Build up a 9-month supply of food, water and supplies at your home and Bug Out location.
- o Build up a year supply of food, water and supplies at your home and Bug Out location.